Photograph of
Georges Braque
c. 1958

# BRAQUE

*"The spectator who looks at a painting follows the same path as the artist and, since the path is more important than the object itself, the journey is what concerns us most."*

Georges Braque

Georges Braque, one of the co-founders of Cubism along with Picasso, was born in Argenteuil-sur-Seine on 13 May 1882; his father was a house painter and decorator and an amateur artist himself. In 1890 the family moved to Le Havre, a bustling and picturesque port which impressed the young Braque. Nine years later Georges briefly entered his father's decorating business; experiences there influenced his later techniques. He also took flute lessons with Gaston Dufy, where he met and befriended his brother Raoul Dufy, who became a painter too.

Braque attended the town's art school but soon found it too parochial for him.

In 1900 he moved to Paris, where he studied at the private Académie Humbert and then the Ecole des Beaux-Arts, setting up his own studio four years later. About then he made friends with Othon Friesz and Francis Picabia, two other radical young painters. Braque divided his time between work, study and museums. Museum visits were traditional, almost obligatory, for a young artist who was expected - and usually wished - to study the art of the past to enrich his own work. Braque at this time was attracted above all by classical Greek art and that of ancient Egypt, besides famous French masters such as Nicolas Poussin and Jean-Baptiste Corot. Later, Braque would turn to Poussin and Corot, because their works embodied the calm lucidity typical of the French classical tradition. In contemporary art he admired Impressionists such as Monet.

Artistic Paris around 1900 was far from being devoted to calm classicism, however. This was perhaps the most revolutionary period in all art history, marked by violent clashes of critical opinion and dramatic gestures by the avant-garde of the School of Paris. Braque himself, although never an ostentatious person, soon became dissatisfied with the arid academic teachings of the schools.

In 1905, when Braque was 23 and his style was still unformed, friends took him to the Fauvist Exhibition at the Salon d'Automne, where Matisse was exhibiting. (Fauve, meaning wild animal, was the abusive term a critic had hurled at these revolutionaries). Braque was overwhelmed; "Matisse opened the road for me," he wrote 50 years

Braque being visited by Picasso in his studio in Vallauris in 1954, photographed by Lee Miller

later. "What impressed me about Fauvism was its novelty...it was full of fervour, which suited me." During the next two years he attached himself to the Fauvists, producing works like The Decorated Boats (page 4), burning with colours.

By 1907, the biggest single influence on him was the austere, solid, mature art of Paul Cézanne, greatest of the Post-Impressionists, who had died the year before. Braque became obsessed by Cézanne's powerfully structured works, painting landscapes like La Ciotat (page 8).

In October 1907, the poet Guillaume Apollinaire took him to Picasso's studio, the Bateau Lavoir. There he saw Picasso's recently completed Les Demoiselles D'Avignon, the first outburst of a totally new way of painting. The effect on Braque was overwhelming and he began to rethink his own ideas. Picasso and Braque, exact contemporaries, later became friends. Helped by the untiring propaganda on their behalf by the perceptive Apollinaire, they jointly developed one of the first schools of abstract art in Europe - Cubism.

Braque's admiration for Picasso was so great that the following year, influenced by the Spanish

artist, he painted his first large-scale landscape composed of geometric shapes: Houses In L'Estaque (page 8). He became a frequent visitor to the Bateau Lavoir studio, where he was present at the great banquet organised in honour of Le Douanier Rousseau in 1908. Apollinaire introduced Braque's "cubes" to an art dealer named Daniel-Henri Kahnweiler in 1908. These were paintings which had been dismissed by critics and refused admission by the Salon d'Automne. It was also Apollinaire who first called the intellectual search for the deconstruction of objects "Analytical Cubism".

Cubism was created jointly by Braque and Picasso, working as equals, yet the flamboyant Picasso, with his many mistresses, picturesque lifestyle and general flair for self-publicity, took most of the glory. Braque's sober, cool, distinctly French works, such as Violin And Jug (page 10) attracted less attention, as did his private life. He married Marcelle Lapré in 1912 and remained with her all his life; but, for Braque

The painter in his studio, c. 1912

more than most painters, private life was subsumed by art.

Both the pioneers of Cubism aimed to depict objects from the inside, as they really were, not as they appeared from the outside at a particular time and place. They broke down the objects they painted into a multiplicity of facets, so that many different aspects of an object could be viewed simultaneously. Form was not destroyed but rather reorganised in new and complex ways on the picture surfaces. Many critics were baffled but this did not worry Braque and Picasso, who saw themselves as heroic pioneers. Braque took part in the *Blaue Reiter* Exhibition in Munich in 1911, when Kandinsky and others unveiled their own, perhaps even more radical versions of abstract art.

He now felt the need to re-introduce bits of reality onto his canvas: "I wanted to make the sense of touch part of the work of art... That is how I introduced sand, saw-dust and iron filings into my paintings..." In this use of papiers collés, or of pieces of newspaper, imitation wood or marble stuck on canvas, Braque was the pioneer.

When the First World War broke out in 1914, Braque was called up. After being seriously wounded in the head in 1915, he had to undergo trepanation (a skull operation). His return to full health took several years. For a while he continued with Cubism. Little by little, however, Braque's painting became freer, more flexible, and more receptive to new external experiences and emotions.

During the 1920s there was a widespread passion for primitive art, negro masks and early sculptures. The desire for expression in other artistic forms was realised in theatre, ballet and music. Braque always had a special rapport with music, which gave a flexible rhythm to his strokes as in *Still Life With Musical Instruments* (page 16).

In 1922, he was honoured by an exhibition at the Salon d'Automne, which had once rejected him.

Fox, 1911 - watercolour, 65 x 50 cm

He then moved into a calm and well-lit house in the Parc Montsouris he had designed himself; in 1928, instead of going south to Provence as usual, he returned to the Normandy of his boyhood and bought a house at Varangeville near Dieppe, which became his summer home. By this time, Braque had adopted a more pictorial approach, returning to the ancient objects he had admired in the Louvre. In his great still lifes Braque evoked the classical tradition, as in *The Painter And His Model* (page 24) or in the numerous designs he did for ballets like *Les Facheux* (below).

Throughout the Second World War, apart from a brief exile in the Pyrenees during the German occupation, he remained in Paris. He continued to work, producing simple still lifes such as *The Billiard Table* (page 26) which are seen as being in the great classical French tradition. The end of the war was the beginning of a new period of experimentation and hope for Braque, despite recurrent illnesses. His last period dealt with birds in flight, their wings spread towards the realms of freedom as in *On The Wing* (page 26). He also decorated the ceiling of the Etruscan Room in the Louvre with frescoes on the bird theme.

However, old age and illness finally caught up with him; during the last ten years of his life he seldom worked on large scale projects. He devoted himself instead to the illustration of books of poems, such as *The Order Of The Birds*, by Saint-John Perse. Revered and respected, but still aloof and reserved, Braque died in Paris on 31 August 1963.

One of the drawings for a naiad for Diaghilev's ballet Les Facheux, with music by Georges Auric, 1923, Hartford, Wadsworth Athenaeum

# THE DECORATED BOATS

1906 - Oil on canvas, 50.5 x 61.5 cm
Basle, Öffentliche Kunstsammlung

**"It** is impossible just to imitate if one truly wants to create."

The author's short, incisive comments, mostly taken from his *Cahiers* (notebooks) reveal how his creative process worked - his drawings, paintings, engravings and sculptures were the fruits of a logical process, not the random scattering of objects which they sometimes appear to be.

The two greatest masters of 20th century art, Matisse and Picasso, admired and respected, but did not really influence, each other. For Braque, however, the influence of Matisse and the other Fauvists, whose works he first saw at their 1905 exhibition, was powerful if short-lived. Fauvism used intensely vivid colours in a non-natural way, but produced recognisable forms. "Fauvist painting was exciting and suited my youth (I was then 23)... As I did not like Romanticism, this physical way of painting pleased me. However the novelty soon faded. I saw that its feverish intensity could not last... I saw that there was something else." (Braque, *Painting And Ourselves, Cahiers d'Art,* 1954). That "something else" was his new concept of reality, his interest no longer being in superficial appearances, but in the essence or even the idea of things. This painting of the port of Antwerp demonstrates his link with Fauvism and the pictorial experiments which he and his friend Othon Friesz made in the summer of 1906 in the Belgian town. The capturing of the vibrant light through quick brush strokes of

colour and carefully chosen combinations of tones produce an effect of luminous transparency and intense depth. The painting is far removed from his later rejection of colour in favour of ochre and sepia tones. Even so, in the strong contours of the planes and the vibrancy of colour, the characteristics of his later works and mature art can be recognised.

*Othon Friesz: The Port Of Antwerp, 1906 - Oil on canvas, 60.5 x 73 cm - Paris, Private collection. This picture, painted during a stay in Antwerp with Braque, reflects experiments with Fauvism in the lively, vibrantly matching colour tones.*

*The Bateaux- Lavoirs, 1902 - Sepia on paper, 15 x 24.8 cm - Paris, Collection M. and Mme. Laurens. This watercolour depicts the studio-boats of the painters floating on the Seine. Braque has outlined their silhouettes against the distant arches of the bridge using an almost pointillist technique. His fondness for head-on views and a lateral use of space is apparent here.*

# SEATED WOMAN

1907 - Oil on canvas, 55 x 46 cm
Paris, Centre Georges Pompidou

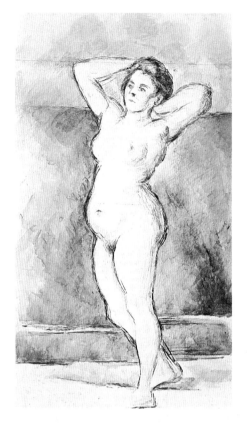

"The limitation of means defines a style, engenders new forms and incites to creation."

This picture reveals the influence of Cézanne's art, already beginning to eclipse that of the Fauvists. Just before meeting Picasso, while he was still half under the influence of the Fauvists Henri Matisse and André Derain, Braque had experimented with painting nudes. He was more interested in their expressive nature than in their inherent beauty, reflecting perhaps a certain puritanical - or at least strongly cerebral - streak in his art. The colours in this nude are still basically Fauvist in their warmth and vividness, but the nature of the subject demanded a way of painting that was more concerned with volume and forms than colour. The model is shown from the back, nude from the waist up, combing her hair with her arms raised to her neck. The sharp curve of the chair reinforces the diagonal pose of the body and its roughly painted anatomy. She reveals the influence on Braque of the great masters both of his own time and of earlier periods, most especially Degas. Her attitude and action are both strongly reminiscent of Degas' many nude studies. Braque did not, however, make such nudes studies a recurrent theme in his art.

*Paul Cézanne: Study Of A Nude, c. 1895. - Watercolour on a graphite sketch, 89 x 53 cm - Paris, Musée d'Orsay. Cézanne's new conception of volume and space played a fundamental part in Braque's artistic development. Braque worked further on defining volume, the play of light on the planes, and the weight of the figure, to give his paintings a sculptural power.*

*Large Nude, 1907 - Oil on canvas, 140 x 102 cm - Paris, Gallery Alex Maguy. Here, painted soon after Braque's crucial meeting with Picasso, Cubism is already apparent. The figure appears to merge with the space around it. Here, Braque has abandoned the traditional proportions and tonal harmonies of the Fauvists. The protruding planes are typical of Cubist painting.*

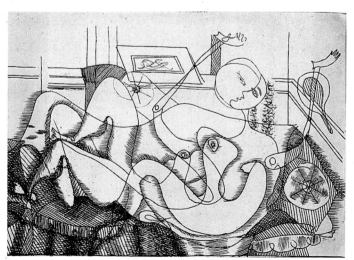

*Reclining Nude, 1934 - Etching, 18 x 30 cm "I must create a new sort of beauty, the beauty which I see in terms of volume, of line, of mass, of weight; through that beauty, I interpret my subjective impression... I want to expose the Absolute, not simply the artificial woman." Here, in a much later painting, the enduring influence of the years of Cubist discovery is still evident.*

# HOUSES IN L'ESTAQUE

1908 - Oil on canvas, 73 x 60 cm
Berne, Kunstmuseum

"The artist is not misunderstood, he is unrecognised.
He is exploited without being known."

L'Estaque in the south of France, with the bulk of its mountains around the bay, inspired Braque when he went there in 1908 and saw the actual landscapes which had enthused both Cézanne and Renoir. There he began a series of pictures in which elements of nature and architecture were intermingled with an almost musical regular rhythm. Tree trunks resembled pillars, while the pure, angular shapes of doorless, windowless houses were arranged in clusters against the cubic hills. Then, little by little, the landscapes became pure compositions, a collection of absolute shapes and masses. In this painting the narrow strip of sky of his early pictures has disappeared and the canvas is filled with merging forms in the synthetic

(artificial) structure of the composition. This was painted using a palette with increasingly sober, dull tones of grey, ochre and opaque green. In this muted, even drab attitude to colour, Braque showed how he was beginning to move away from the influence of Cézanne, who had never totally rejected colour.
"To work from nature is to improvise... I do not copy appearances; appearances are the result. To be pure imitation, painting must disregard appearances." (*Thoughts And Reflections On Painting* in *Nord-Sud*, December 1917).
This extraordinary work, with its marked simplicity and precision of structure, became in effect a manifesto for Cubism.

*Raoul Dufy:* Landscape At L'Estaque, *1908 - Oil on canvas, 73 x 60 cm - Beaulieu-Sur-Mer, private collection. After seeing Matisse's works, Dufy moved from an Impressionist to a Fauvist style. At the same time he came closer to Cézanne's geometric vision, as seen in this landscape, for example. He remained a brilliant colourist; his canvases thrill with the fireworks of his strokes.*

La Ciotat, *1907 - Pittsburgh, private collection. This painting is still influenced by Fauvism, as is apparent from the tones and their combinations. The colours of the trunks, for example, change according to the background, and pass from purplish blue in the foreground to purplish red.*

*Paul Cézanne:* Jourdan's Cottage (unfinished), *1906 - Oil on canvas, 65 x 81 cm - private collection. The masses of the houses, the trees and the space which surrounds them are painted according to his famous principle: "... To treat nature as a cylinder, a sphere, a cone" - that is, as pure forms.*

# VIOLIN AND JUG

1909/1910 - Oil on canvas, 117 x 73.5 cm
Basle, Kunstmuseum

"There is no imitating appearances; appearances are results.
The senses deform, the mind forms."

The diagram reveals the outlines which, through the breakdown of the planes, suggest the presence of the objects portrayed - the jug and the violin.

This picture, painted in the winter of 1909/10, shows that Braque's collaboration with Picasso was beginning to bear fruit. Their parallel lines of art now converged. There is a greater fragmentation and disintegration of form here. Braque wrote: "With this subject, it is as if a fog has lifted and objects have emerged...When fragmented objects appeared in my painting in 1909, it was a method of getting as close as possible to the object... Fragmentation helped me to establish space and movement in space. I could only introduce the object after having created the space for it..."

This was the "analytical phase" (the poet Apollinaire's phrase) of Cubism which followed the three-dimensional Cézannesque period.

It was characterised by the decomposition of volume (or mass) into facets (or planes) which were broken down and then overlapped on other planes, which had often been superimposed. The forms which had been broken down were then rearranged in new ways through a complex interplay of their surfaces. This produces the broken, jagged-rock effect typical of some aspects of Cubist painting; it also gives the impression that the onlooker can reassemble a picture from its separate pieces.

Braque's coolly cerebral work always contrasted with the dramatic violence of Picasso's. In this picture, the planes create facets which seem to emit a mysterious, soft silvery light in their transparency.

Left: Georges Braque, The Violin - 1911, Oil on canvas, 73 x 60 cm Lyons, Musée des Beaux-Arts.
Right: Pablo Picasso: The Violin, 1912 - Oil on canvas, 55 x 46 cm Moscow, Pushkin Museum. Both Picasso and Braque, while experimenting with the breakdown of mass and volume, enjoyed painting in oval forms. However, while the former developed a more dramatic approach, the latter opted for an increasing tonal harmony.

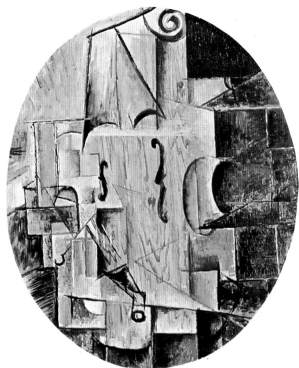

# PEDESTAL TABLE

1913 - Oil on canvas, 65 x 92 cm
Basle, Öffentliche Kunstsammlung

"**W**ork to perfect the mind.
There is no certainty
except in what is conceived
by the mind."

Braque was indisputably the first to use letters of the alphabet and large printed numbers directly on his canvases. He then added pieces of simulated marble or wood onto them. These new elements gave the pictures a new and more tangible feel; they also served as ways of conjuring up most vividly the essence of the real world.
"While still trying to get as close as possible to reality, I introduced letters into my paintings in 1911. They were forms which could not be distorted because, being flat shapes, the letters were outside its space, and their presence in the painting, by contrast, allowed me to distinguish objects within its space from those outside it."
Given this kind of approach, it is not surprising that the artist renounced colour in an attempt to avoid distracting himself from seeing and grasping space. Colour played such a minor role in his work at this stage that at times it seems to have vanished altogether and the onlooker is left facing a drab monochrome wash. It was essentially the aspects of light which interested the artist.
"It is a fact which critics have never fully understood. This is how colour became divorced from form and their independence from each other became obvious... Colour works simultaneously with form, but they have in reality nothing to do with each other."

*Guitar And Clarinet, 1918 - Charcoal and gouache, imitation wood, coloured paper and corrugated cardboard stuck on grey-blue cardboard, 77 x 95 cm - Philadelphia, Museum of Art. This picture may appear at first sight far removed from a still-life by Cézanne but, remembering the Cubist desire to "deconstruct" reality, it can be seen as a still life executed in another language. According to Cubist syntax, the use of unusual materials created a novel relationship between the objects represented.*

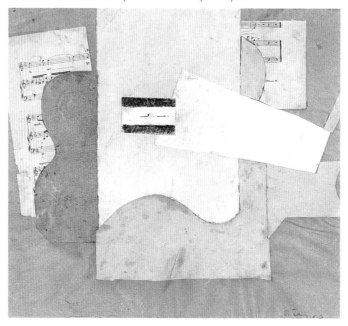

*Pablo Picasso: Sheet Of Music And Guitar, 1912/13 - collage, 42.5 x 48 cm - Paris, Georges Salles collection. At the start of 1912, Picasso, following Braque, produced his first collages. In contrast with Braque, Picasso used this new technique in his paintings as well as his drawings.*

# WOMAN WITH GUITAR

1913 - Oil on canvas, 130 x 74 cm
Paris, Centre Georges Pompidou

"**N**ature does not give us the taste for perfection.
It does not distinguish between better or worse."

Musical instruments feature again and again in Braque's works, testimony both to his own deep musical interests and to their pictorial qualities (they make good subjects for a painting). They create another link between Braque's work and the French tradition of still lifes going back to the 17th century. "I painted a lot of musical instruments at that time, first because I was surrounded by them, and secondly because their shape and volume fell into in the field of still life, as I understood the term. I was aiming for tactile, touchable space, as I like to define it, and the musical instrument as an object came to life when touched."
1910 marked the end of a period when Braque used simple planes in his pictures. Cubism then evolved towards an explosion of forms in a myriad facets. These intermingled more and more freely, making the subject all but disappear in favour of a nearly monochrome structure, based on ochres, greys and earth colours. This was the period of Analytic Cubism.
It was followed in 1912-13 by the period of Synthetic (artificial) Cubism where the painter worked on a synthetic reconstruction of the object by introducing meaning, colour and materials, such as stuck-on paper and type characters. All processes of imitation had by now been abandoned; the object was represented by the breakdown of its masses and the multiplicity of points of view, to be reconstructed freely on the space of the canvas. In *Woman With Guitar*, the severely-structured wide rectangular planes

contrast with the collage background. The brown imitation wood of the body of the guitar and the back of the armchair stand out against the monotonous colour tones. It is the fruit of an intellectual pursuit which aimed to make the actual substance of a picture of total importance.

*Opposite: This diagram shows the horizontal lines which divide the area of the painting into three bands, and the vertical and diagonal lines which, in crossing them, suggest the woman's figure, her head, her facial features, her torso, and her hands, as well as the presence of a guitar. The division of the space is reinforced by the idea of using words as a point of reference.*

Woman With Guitar (after Corot), 1923 - Oil on canvas, 41 x 33 cm - Paris, Centre Georges Pompidou. This painting, inspired by Corot's Portrait Of Christine Nilsson, is a variation on one of the favourite themes of the painter, whom Braque admired enormously.

Pablo Picasso: Woman With Mandolin, 1909 - Oil on canvas, 92 x 73 cm - Leningrad, Hermitage Museum. This painting shows the start of the period when Braque and Picasso followed similar paths; they both sought to go beyond mere appearances to get to the core of objects

# THE MUSICIAN

1917/18 - Oil on canvas, 221.5 x 113 cm
Basle, Öffentliche Kunstsammlung

"The painter thinks in terms of forms and colours; objects are his poetics."

This shows Braque beginning to regain his taste for colour. Dating from the end of the First World War, when Braque had taken up Cubism again after his long convalescence, it has far more colour than his earlier Cubist works. The mosaic at the bottom glitters with tiny blue and gold points, rather like bathroom decorations. The legacy of his brief apprenticeship with his father, an interior decorator and furniture restorer, surfaces here perhaps. Braque's innovative strength lay basically in the pursuit of a new quality of space which was not based on illusion (as art had been, since the Renaissance perfected the techniques of making a two-dimensional flat canvas give the illusion of a third dimension). He replaced traditional perspective with a vision made from several points of view, "dismantling" it so as to rebuild it in an ideal way on a two-dimensional surface from an overall geometry of form. In doing this the space and the object joined and fitted together.

For this reason the objects chosen by Braque and Picasso for their Cubist experiments were deliberately simple, since they could easily be dismantled, easily recognised and - this was the theory - reconstructed by the eager observer. Hence the musician here is to be reconstructed from the fragments of his shoe or eye.

*Opposite: Pablo Picasso, Harlequin, 1915 - Oil on canvas, 183 x 105 cm - New York, Museum of Modern Art. This is a charming painting, with its multicoloured costume and melancholic figure, noticeable above all for the Cubist treatment of the depiction, with its displaced, cut-out planes lightly pivoting on each other.*

*Below: Still Life With Musical Instruments, 1908 - Oil on canvas, 50 x 61 cm - Paris, Collection M. and Mme Claude Laurens. This painting was considered by Braque to be his first truly Cubist piece: the one in which a new tactile and visual space was created without using illusionistic perspective. It introduced the musical instruments he kept in his studio and liked to play. Planes open up or tilt, already showing more of the object than actually visible from any one viewpoint.*

# STILL LIFE WITH A GUITAR

1921 - Oil on canvas, 60 x 100 cm
Prague, Narodni Gallery

"The artist must not be asked for more than he can give, just as one cannot ask the critic for more than he can see. We do not try to convince, but are content to provoke thought."

Between 1921 and 1927 Braque painted a whole series of *Mantelpiece* canvases; these presented still-life elements in a horizontal or vertical format. In these he managed to combine the established mode of Cubist painting with the new, more naturalistic mode of the post-war years, slowly and subtly increasing the elements of space and depth in his pictures. The textures here are extremely varied: rough and smooth planes, marble veining, spotted and mottled strips, which have been painted in trompe-l'oeil, a skill Braque had acquired in adolescence as a decorator. Running through this still-life can be seen lines reminiscent of music staves; the letters half-hidden by the guitar, which is the dominating feature of the piece, spell out the word *Quatuor* (quartet). In another similar piece in the same museum (right), this time in a vertical format, the word *Valse* (waltz) can be discerned. Braque's new pictorial concept in the 1920s was based on the complete involvement of the observer. It called on the sense of sight, but also of touch, to piece together the elements of the picture. This process took place through intellectual stimulation.
Braque also insisted on the poetic dimension of the composition: "Reality is only revealed when illuminated by a poetic ray.

The Fireplace, *1920/21 - Oil on canvas, 130 x 75 cm - Prague, Narodni Gallery. Synthetic Cubism attempted to restructure the pictorial vision by combining its geometric, and therefore unreal volumes, with very real subject matter. This is also sometimes called Valse - a refference to the music score above the fireplace.*

The Marble Table, *1925 - Oil on canvas, 130 x 74 cm - Paris, Centre Georges Pompidou. This painting depicts the Synthetic solution of the two themes explored by Braque during this period: pedestal tables and fireplaces. The still life is raised on a circular table-top covered by a white tablecloth, shaded in with black.*

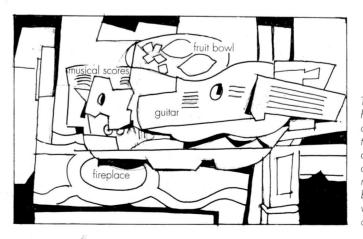

*The diagram shows the horizontal composition of the image seen from the front and from above. The objects are arranged on the mantelpiece, outlined by thick, sinuous outlines which soften the rigidity of the Cubist structure.*

Everything is dormant around us." This "poetic ray" succeeded in ennobling the most banal of subjects, giving them an absolute, universal dimension, according to Braque's theory. It was this phenomenon which Cubism used to introduce a new relationship between art and reality.

Meanwhile the Futurist movement, which was developing at more or less the same time in Italy, introduced objects onto the canvas suggesting modernity, such as machines, cars, trains and aeroplanes. By contrast, the Cubists portrayed modest, universally known objects which people were used to seeing in their houses. They were therefore easy to recognise and reconstruct: tables, jugs, musical instruments and glasses, to which were added human figures in everyday poses. In this painting a guitar, a fruit bowl and a paper are seen placed on the marble mantelpiece. There is a harmony of dull, muted tones: the yellow and brown of the guitar, the green of the fruit and parts of the background, and the grey of the stone of the chimney.

*Pablo Picasso: Fruit Bowl And Guitar, 1924 - Zurich, Kunsthaus. For Picasso, Cubism was simply one way among many others, such as neoclassicism, of expressing his feelings. The subject of a picture had little real importance for him. He said: "I do not know in advance what I am going to put on the canvas, just as I do not know in advance which colours I will use."*

*Juan Gris: The Blue Carpet, 1925 - Paris, Centre Georges Pompidou. Braque often explored the theme of a still life placed on a wooden table, often covered by a white or coloured tablecloth with strong black shadows. The same theme was taken up by Picasso, Matisse and Juan Gris, as in this painting where the objects stand out from and match the colour of the carpet. But Gris' method was different: "Cézanne makes a cylinder out of a bottle, whereas I go from a cylinder to paint a bottle. Cézanne moves towards architecture, whereas I move away from it." Gris proceeded from the form to the subject. His vibrant, brilliant colours are in marked contrast to the dingy tones Braque normally preferred.*

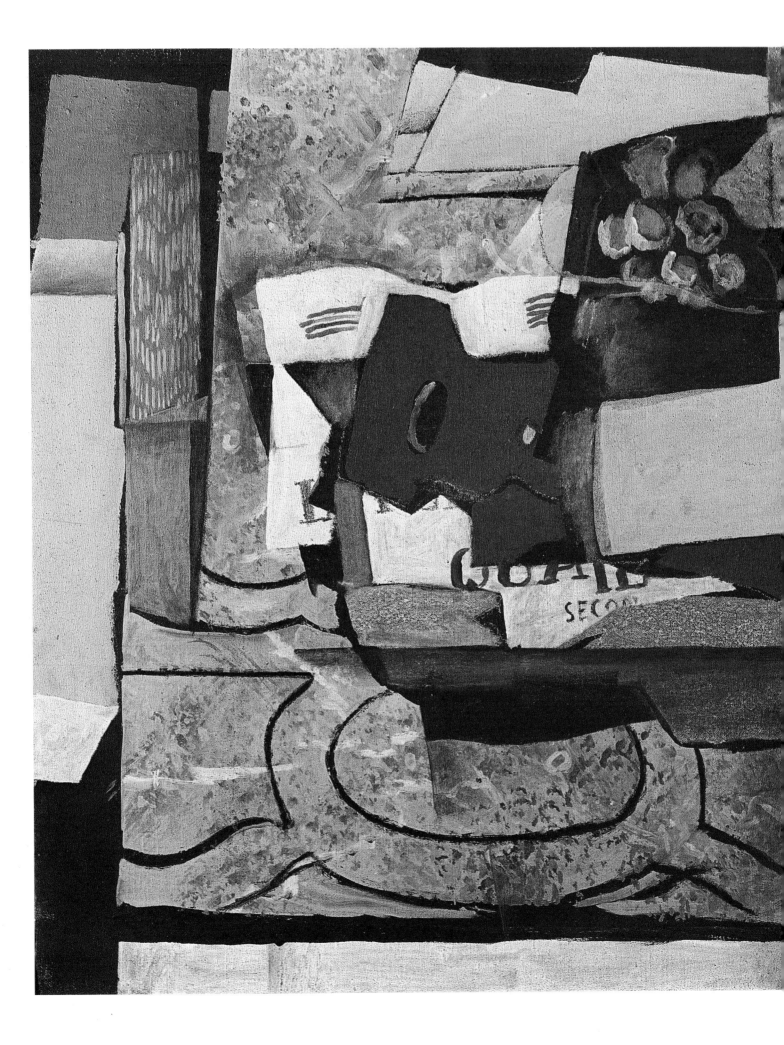

# THE LARGE GUERIDON (PEDESTAL TABLE)

1929 · Oil on canvas, 145 x 114 cm
Washington, Phillips Collection

"A still life ceases to be a still life when it is out of reach."

This is one of a series of large-scale *Guéridon* or *Table* pictures. The pedestal table motif was dear to Braque. He originally used it in 1911 and went back to it over a period of 40 years. This painting is the most important in this series.

These works show a total change in Braque's handling of materials, colour and space. The previous black grounds (painted bases) are replaced by a grainy coating of a mixture of plaster and sand, which appears matt, covered by a film of paint, similar to a fresco. More is revealed of the space around the subject, now visible between the baseboard and the ceiling.

In this *Guéridon,* Braque innovated by setting the table in the corner of two walls, which meet at right angles. This is the most complex, most colourful and triumphantly successful of the four *Guéridons.* Here Braque, far more than he had ever done previously, emphasised the solidity of the table base. He has kept the picture flat and yet made the table and still life on top of it appear extremely strong.

"I take the greatest care with the background of my canvases, because the background supports all the rest, just like the foundations of a house. I have always been very preoccupied with the subject because there is as much sensitivity in the technique as in the rest of the painting. I prepare and grind the colours myself."

The nature and quality of the background from which the objects spring are fundamentally important in Braque's composition.

The Red Guéridon, *1939/52 Oil on canvas, 180 x 73 cm - Paris, Centre Georges Pompidou. This painting, which Braque worked on for over ten years, is the opulent conclusion of the series started in 1911. It is striking in the richness of its colours and the strength of its structure.*

*Gino Severini:* Still Life With The Literary Revue 'Nord-Sud', *1910. Paris, private collection. Gino Severini, who died in Paris in 1956, was the only Italian Futurist artist to have concrete and effective dealings with Cubism. Settling in France in 1906, he followed Synthetic Cubism before he moved on to freer techniques such as collage with painted letters.*

# THE DUO

1937 - Oil on canvas, 130 x 160 cm
Paris, Centre Georges Pompidou

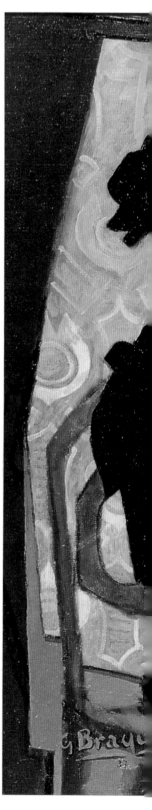

> "All things considered, I prefer those who exploit me to those who follow me. They have something to teach me."

During the mid 1930s, Braque seems to have felt that it was time to animate his heavily decorated interiors and accordingly he reintroduced the human figure into his work on a large scale. Either alone or in couples, they greatly enlivened his paintings, which would have otherwise been plunged into deepest drabness and general obscurity.
As with the objects of his still lives, his characters tended still to become mere silhouettes, as if the mature Braque distrusted anything so straightforwardly sensual as the human body seen in the round.
In this painting, however, Braque has gone some way to reinstating both human figures and a

recognisable, if scarcely conventional, structure to the picture. Around this time Braque began to make his paintings more immediately attractive.
As is obvious from the cover of the score, the couple are playing the music of Claude Debussy, whom Braque greatly admired.
Braque and Debussy, in their respective fields, both represented the pursuit of new forms in their art: Braque through the fragmentation and breakdown of planes, Debussy through the repetition and intermingling of rhythms which echoed each other. Debussy's popular music might seem light years removed from Braque's art, but Braque felt there was a kinship.

The Painter And His Model, *1939 - Oil on canvas, 130 x 176 cm - New York, Walter P. Chrysler Jr. Collection. Here we find the same light and dark silhouettes which define the figures of the painter and his model, but Braque is far more assured by now in his presentation of people. The artist, with his pointed beard, cigarette and ragged hair, has an individual quality most of Braque's figures lack. The model is as impersonal - in a way recalling Egyptian art - as anything Braque ever painted.*

# THE BILLIARD TABLE I

1945 - Oil on canvas, 130.5 x 95.5 cm
Paris, Centre Georges Pompidou

Starting in the autumn of 1944 and finishing in 1949, Braque painted a series of seven pictures, showing billiard tables seen from differing angles and presented either frontally, obliquely or lengthwise. He was fascinated by the table's trapezoid shape and the two-dimensional surface of the canvas, and by the interplay of the colours: the red of the balls and the brown of the table's surround against the green baize. This fascination did not derive from any sporting interest on Braque's part in the game of billiards itself, but rather in the pictorial opportunities a billiard table offered him.

This original version shows *The Billiard Table* obliquely, with the top aligned with the corner of the room. The artist exposes the tabletop to the observer as if it has been tilted to face him.

The heavy structure of the dado and cornices running around the walls, the window bars and the thick wooden frame around the tabletop are architectural details which intensify the impression of a confined and compressed space. The point of view appears to change along the surface of the green cloth. It is renewed by the crossed billiard cues, the asymmetry of the walls, the balance of the windows which frame the layout, and the harmonious transparency of the colour tones.

*The Billiard Table, 1944/52 - Oil on canvas, 195 x 97 cm Mrs Gelman Collection, on loan to the Metropolitan Museum of Art in New York. In this vertical variation on the same theme, the table top is supported on heavy carved legs. The perspective is cut in two by the horizontal fold, marked by a narrowing of the table which pushes the background further away. In the wall mirror in the background a bracket light, a hat rack and a framed painting are clearly visible.*

*Preparatory sketch c. 1944 - Pencil - Paris, Private collection. This demonstrates Braque's conception of space, with the flat surface broken by an imaginary line which separates the different points of view. The curves of the gueridon and the chair next to the billiard table help to accentuate the rectilinear, broken rhythm of the shape of the billiard table.*

"Shape and colour do not merge. They exist
side by side."

# ON THE WING

1956/61 - Oil on canvas, 114.5 x 170.5 cm
Paris, Centre Georges Pompidou

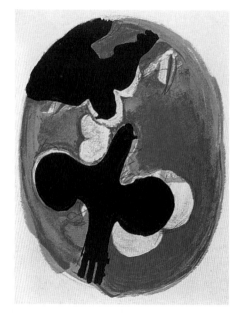

In his last years, although racked by recurrent illnesses, Braque's art turned to a lyrical series of landscapes and bird scenes, both inspired by trips to the marshes of the Camargue in southern France. "Above the marshes I saw great flocks of birds; from this vision I chose their aerial forms. The birds inspired me."

Here he has painted a cloud as a dark, voluminous shape in the centre of a coarsely granular, opaque blue sky. Through it an elongated bird flies slowly and heavily, its sombre solidity giving it the metallic mass of a piece of sculpture. As if offering a mocking echo of its heavy flight, a small bright bird flies in a white frame in the bottom left corner. It is painted using a dense impasto (thickly applied opaque paint).

The dynamics of space which Braque had sought to create through everyday objects now switched to drawings, lithographs, and paintings dedicated to birds. There is a poetic resonance to these last works showing the flight of birds through vast space. Braque said of these paintings: "I do not seek limitation; I seek delimitation".

*Study for the ceiling of the Louvre. These decorations, again on the theme of birds and flight, were among Braque's last works. Remarkably for a sick man in his seventies, he created something fresh, vivid and quite unexpected in his art.*

*Bird Returning To Its Nest, 1955/56 - Oil on canvas, 130 x 173 cm - Paris, Centre Georges Pompidou. This is a mysterious, nocturnal scene. The colours of the bird itself are a muted beige, while its surroundings are in greens and browns so dark that they verge on black. Braque's bird is not simply a symbolic bird, it represents the very principle of movement, the universal symbol of space and freedom. Braque selected this piece to be displayed at the Brussels World Fair in 1958.*

# THE FRENCH CUBIST

Cubism was the shaping influence on Braque's art, even after he had long ago theoretically left it. Rejecting in its typical forms all interest in its subject matter, in themes, history or anecdotes, Cubism restricted itself to a narrow range of still lifes. Indisputably a most important movement in 20th century art, it is also the most limiting and austere. Indeed, Cubism has been described as an artistic corset which most painters were only too glad to shake off.

In Braque's art, however, Cubism's restrictions seemed to leave a permanent and not unwelcome mark. For him Cubism seemed to rephrase in modern terms the austere lessons of the great French tradition of still lifes epitomised by the works of Chardin, the great 18th century painter of still lifes, and Cézanne. These scrupulously observed studies of small details of everyday life - fruit bowls, loaves of bread or bottles of wine, pieces of fish or meat - studiously ignored all grand or facile themes.

It was this approach which first attracted Braque and to which he in some ways returned later in his career. In this he was very different from most members of the polyglot Ecole de Paris (Paris School), led by Picasso, who later branched out in their multifarious ways. Not for Braque a blue or a pink phase, nor a return to the art of antiquity; although his art did soften and mellow perceptibly after 1918, he never indulged in displays of bright colour or illustrated mythical subjects. Only at the end of his life did he relax to paint his lyrical *Flight* series (page 28).

"M. Braque is a very daring young man. The disconcerting influence of Picasso and Derain has made him bolder. Perhaps the style of Cézanne and the memory of the

## BRAQUE AND HIS TIMES

|  | HIS LIFE AND WORKS | HISTORY | ART AND CULTURE |
|---|---|---|---|
| 1882 | Born 13 April at Argenteuil-sur-Seine, son of a house painter | Tuberculosis bacillus discovered<br>Phoenix Park murders in Dublin worsen Anglo-Irish relations<br>Anti-Jewish pogroms in Russia | Death of Charles Darwin<br>Birth of Virginia Woolf and James Joyce<br>Degas: *Women Ironing* |
| 1890 | His family settles in Le Havre; he starts studying at the local Arts School | Cecil Rhodes becomes Prime Minister of Cape Colony, South Africa<br>Parnell Scandal splits Irish Nationalists | Death of Van Gogh<br>Toulouse-Lautrec: *Dance At The Moulin Rouge*<br>Debussy sets *Five Poems* by Baudelaire to music |
| 1899 | He starts work in the family business as a decorator | Rehabilitation of Alfred Dreyfus<br>Start of the Boer War in South Africa | Edward Elgar: *Enigma Variations*<br>W.B. Yeats: *The Wind In The Reeds*<br>Monet: *Water Lilies* |
| 1900 | Moves to Paris to continue his legal studies | World Fair in Paris<br>Boxer rising in China<br>Zeppelin makes first flight by airship | Klimt: *Philosophy*<br>Alfred Jarry: *Ubu Enchained*<br>Triumph of Art Nouveau at Paris World Fair<br>Elgar: *The Dream of Gerontius* |
| 1902 | After doing his military service, he joins the Académie Humbert before studying briefly at the Académie des Beaux-Arts | End of the Boer War<br>Italy leaves the Triple Alliance with Austria and Germany<br>Education Act extends compulsory secondary schooling in England | Henry James: *The Wings Of The Dove*<br>Rudyard Kipling: *Just So Stories*<br>Arthur Conan Doyle: *The Hound of The Baskervilles*<br>André Gide: *The Immoralist* |
| 1905 | He is overwhelmed by the Fauvist Exhibition at the Salon d'Automn; starts to paint under their influence | Russians accept defeat by Japanese and cede Manchuria<br>"Bloody Sunday" in Saint Petersburg triggers revolutions throughout Russia | Paul Cézanne: *Les Grandes Baigneuses*<br>Birth of Anthony Powell and Kenneth Clark<br>Albert Einstein: *Theory Of Relativity* |
| 1907 | Stays in the south of France where he paints canvases marked by Cézanne's influence. Meets Picasso; fascinated by *Les Demoiselles d'Avignon* | Rasputin establishes himself at the Court of the Tsar<br>Triple Entente of Britain, France and Russia formed | Birth of W.H. Auden<br>Kipling wins Nobel Prize for literature<br>James Joyce: *Chamber Music* |
| 1908 | Exhibits at Kahnweiller (*Houses At L'Estaque*); the critic Louis Vauxcelles talks of Braque's "cubes." Cubism is born | Austria annexes Bosnia<br>Asquith becomes Prime Minister<br>Pensions Act establishes first state pensions in Britain | E. M. Forster: *Room With A View*<br>Kandinsky: *Landscape With Towers*<br>Ezra Pound: *A Lume Spento*<br>Bonnard: *Nude Against The Light* |

static art of the Egyptians also pre-occupy him to excess. He creates terribly simplistic, distorted metallic figures. He has little respect for form, he reduces everything, including figures and houses, to geometric diagrams or cubes. Let us not scoff, however, because he has good intentions. And let us wait." So wrote the critic Louis de Vauxcelles after seeing the exhibition at the Kahnweiller Gallery in Paris in November 1908. In this he displayed unusual perceptiveness, most uncommon among the generally hostile ranks of critics. These had scarcely got used to the vague dap-plings of the Impressionists and were still puzzling over the stark forms of the Post-Impressionists, especially Paul Cézanne.

In 1907 Braque himself had been tremendously impressed by a major Cézanne retrospective in Paris. He started to paint in a style clearly influenced by the reclusive Provençal, whose works had only fairly recently become widely known. Braque regarded Cézanne as the true master of volume and mass and tried to follow his geometrical analysis of objects. This is shown both by nudes such as *Seated Woman* (page 6) or *Houses At L'Es-taque* (page 8), a landscape which pays homage to Cézanne's monumental (imposing in a solid, sometimes massive but not necessarily large way) works.

*Houses At L'Estaque* also reveals another, more explosive influence - that of Picasso's *Les Demoiselles D'Avignon*. This extraordinary work, which Picasso showed Braque on his first visit to his studio in 1907, seemed to Braque to be destined to carry on where Cézanne had left off, looking at nature in terms of spheres, cubes and cylinders. *Les Demoiselles* was a violent revolt against both traditional

| Year | | | |
|------|---|---|---|
| 1912 | Marries Marcelle Lapré. Stays at Sorgues with Picasso where he creates his first collages. Exhibits with the Munich Secession | Start of the Balkan Wars as Turkish empire collapses<br>Irish Home Rule Bill passed but shelved at outbreak of war | Marc Chagall: *Homage To Apollinaire*<br>Fernand Leger: *Woman In Blue*<br>Birth of Lawrence Durrell<br>Lutyens builds Castle Drogo |
| 1915 | Wounded on the front in Artois in May. Says in hospital until June 1916 | Turks massacre one million Armenians<br>Italy enters war on side of the Allies<br>Gallipoli campaign fails | Joyce: *Portrait Of The Artist As A Young Man*<br>Amedeo Modigliani: *Beatrice Hastings*<br>D.W. Griffith: *Birth Of A Nation* |
| 1922 | He abandons the strictest rigidity of Cubism | Mussolini marches on Rome and sets up dictatorship<br>Lloyd George falls from power; Liberal Party splits | Joyce: *Ulysees*<br>T.S. Eliot: *The Waste Land*<br>Birth of Kingsley Amis<br>Lutyens building New Delhi |
| 1928 | Begins a new series of *Guéridons*. Starts spending the summer at Varangeville | Discovery of penicillin by Alexander Fleming<br>Fifth Reform Act gives all women over 21 the vote | D.H.Lawrence: *Lady Chatterley's Lover*<br>Virginia Woolf: *Orlando*<br>Stanley Spencer painting the frescoes at Burghclerc |
| 1938 | He starts the series of *Studios* which are interrupted by the war | Hitler annexes Austria<br>Munich Crisis: Neville Chamberlain hands over half Czechoslovakia to Hitler<br>Wave of anti-Jewish pogroms in Germany | Jean Cocteau: *Les Parents Terribles*<br>George Orwell: *Homage to Catalonia*<br>Lawrence Durrell: *The Black Book* |
| 1942 | Spends the war in Paris, oppressed by the German occupation | Wannsee Conference; Nazis decide to murder all Jews<br>Battles of Stalingrad and El Alamein halt German offensives | Albert Camus: *The Outsider*<br>Death of Walter Sickert |
| 1949 | After winning a prize at the Venice Biennale, he starts a new series of paintings dealing with birds | End of Berlin airlift<br>Creation of NATO<br>Communists win civil war in China and proclaim People's Republic | Jorge Luis Borges: *Aleph*<br>George Orwell: *1984*<br>Osbert Sitwell: *Laughter In The Next Room* |
| 1963 | Dies in Paris 31 August | Macmillan resigns as Prime Minister after the Profumo scandal<br>President Kennedy assassinated; Johnson succeeds him and continues US build-up in Vietnam | Death of Jean Cocteau and Aldous Huxley<br>Luchino Visconti: *The Leopard*<br>Anthony Burgess: *Inside Mr Enderby* |

and Impressionist treatments of form. The two young artists felt very strongly that the Impressionists in particular had neglected form in favour of colour. The figures of *Les Demoiselles,* still recognisable as such, seem to break out of the flat plane of the canvas into the third dimension in a half-sculptural manner, which is what Cubism wished to depict on canvas.

## CO-FOUNDERS OF CUBISM

Braque and Picasso from now on worked together with unflagging energy. Picasso later declared that: "When we created Cubism, we had no intention of doing so; we were trying only to express what was within us". Each artist followed the dictates of his own personality and his own sense of direction. In contrast to Picasso, Braque was not passionate or violent in his work. Always moving on, Braque searched for new aesthetic, poetic and psychological concepts which could give form and body to his sensations. In short, Braque was lucid, coolly level-headed and systematic. By contrast Picasso, driven by his passionate, fiery instincts, did not seek out the diffuse notes of muted colouring in his cubes. Instead, he sought a style based more on form and basically connected to the substance of the shapes.

The two friends and rivals, Braque and Picasso, had such a constant exchange of experiments and close collaboration, together with their common reference to Cézanne, that neither artist can claim real precedence in Cubism's invention. In fact, priority would be impossible to attribute for, although the two artists' work is close, it is also very different.

In 1917, Braque began to keep his *Cahiers,* a series of notebooks in which he recorded his methods and which he continued to keep throughout his life. It reveals the calm, rational progress of his art. He wrote: "I wish to be at one with nature, rather than to copy it. I am not a revolutionary painter. I do not seek exaltation. Enthusiasm is enough for me." He also wrote: "I do not want to distort, I take what is around and had courage enough to take a stand with regard to the shapeless and to form it." The forms he used were not only cuboid, he also returned, after his recovery from his head wound in 1915, to the use of sinuous lines and ovals. With his use of the oval, Braque showed once again that he was more interested in a picture's surface than in the exploration of volume.

His use of collage, putting fragments of material onto a painting, is indisputably a first. He wished painting to be autonomous and at the same time to represent the actual idea of reality by way of a few details which made it recognisable. Undoubtedly memories of his father's craft as house painter, furniture restorer and decorator, at which he himself had worked for a while, influenced Braque's invention of collage. Picasso was to go further, by adding more complex and varied bits of material so that he made a veritable collection in his paintings.

The difference between the two artists was clearly described by Ardengo Soffici, one of the first intellectuals who understood Cubism and its two principle exponents. In an article in *La Voce* of 24 April 1911, he wrote: "Certainly, Braque does not have the versatility which makes Picasso a phenomenal living summary of ten years of pictorial research; but on the other hand, how much love, intensity and delicacy there is in his work, particularly the more recent pieces! Still lifes depicting a conglomeration of everyday objects on a table, musical instruments, apples, cloths and crockery, and bowls full of fruit, in which the facets of glass, the glint of the wood and marquetry, and the positioning of the material create a prismatic magic which brings to mind the solitude of the alpine glaciers. It is this love and this delicacy which differentiates the Frenchman from the Spaniard. Picasso, full of spirit and burning with an almost barbaric fire, captures the muted violence of drama in the sombre tones and the seemingly algebraic design of his paintings. With his hardly less rigorous technique, Braque obtains a kind of musical calm filled with a cool light. However both of them, without betraying their respective origins, have founded a school of art which is not easy to understand, but which is worthy and has a glorious future ahead of it."

## CHARDIN'S HEIR?

That reference to music was significant, for Braque was keenly musical and kept musical instruments around his studio and house, for use as well as for decoration. These figure prominently as early as *Still Life With Musical Instruments* (page 16) and continue with *Woman With Guitar* (page 14) and *The Musician* (page 16). Such small, domestic details recall to some observers the perfect yet simple still lifes of Chardin, translated into modern terms. These, too, were very different from Picasso's later multifarious developments.

The artistic collaboration of the two friends ended with the First World War; then the diverging sensibilities and choices of the artists drove them apart. Braque enriched his palette, but never allowed colour to become too powerful. His forms later became softer and more sinuous (as in his *Bird* series page 28) and he began to accentuate the decorative tone of the composition, always with the same concern: to separate colour from form and space, so that it would allow the actual spirit of the object to shine through.